MW00699358

Apronisms

**Also by
EllynAnne Geisel**

The Apron Book

Apronisms

Pocket Wisdom for Every Day

By EllynAnne Geisel
A Lark Production

Andrews McMeel
Publishing, LLC

Kansas City

08 09 10 11 12 TEP 10 9 8 7 6 5 4 3 2 1

ISBN-13: 978-0-7407-7124-8
ISBN-10: 0-7407-7124-8

Library of Congress Control Number: 2007934892

www.andrewsmcmeel.com

ATTENTION: SCHOOLS AND BUSINESSES
Andrews McMeel books are available at quantity discounts
with bulk purchase for educational, business, or sales
promotional use. For information, please write to: Special
Sales Department, Andrews McMeel Publishing, LLC,
4520 Main Street, Kansas City, Missouri 64111.

aph•o•rism 1. A concise statement of a principle. 2. A terse formulation of a truth or sentiment.

—Merriam-Webster's 11th Collegiate Dictionary

*A*prons stir up memories of home, motherhood, and love. Reminders of recipes, relationships, and holidays, aprons are homemade icons that represent a family's history. Aprons

tie us all together. You know how the flotsam and jetsam of daily living finds its way into your aprons—scraps of paper with important phone numbers, a special shell, some loose change, the lost earring, rubber bands, and LEGO blocks. So it just makes sense to look to our apron strings and apron pockets for little hints on how to savor and enjoy each day.

The following pages are inspired by the value I find in life's details and my love of a good aphorism. I wanted to share some of the thoughts, observations, advice, and tips I've gathered over the years and put them all in one place, like one big apron pocket. From the specific to the impressionistic, the ideas are now collected here for safekeeping in your own heart.

Dream big, but furnish your castle in the sky room by room.

*D*ream it. Believe it. Then work your patootie off every single day, and you just might achieve it. Take one step at a time toward the goal.

1

Change the dish towel.

Hang a fresh towel and your kitchen will look neater and cleaner, even when it isn't! Note the satisfaction you feel when draping an ironed towel on the oven door. Vintage tea towels. Embroidered beauties. Simple renewal.

What better way to wait for the timer to ding than to sample the batter? When my children were around, I was the model, unselfish mommy who gave each child a beater to lick clean. But now that

nk until you've each had a lick.

my sons have flown the coop, I lick
one beater and save the other for
my husband. Be sure to leave plenty
of batter on the beaters to make the
licking worthwhile. What's the fun
without yum?

Slow dancing in
life isn't the same
as waltzing
through it.

*L*ife is a dance, sometimes fast
paced with challenges, sometimes
stable as a glide. To waltz through life is
to pass by without taking notice; to slow
dance means to savor, observe, relish,
experience, and share. Remember the
days when we strolled babies, walked
at a mosey, and rode bikes at a toodle?
Take time to slow dance.

Be a spendthrift when it comes to kindness and a miser with criticism.

After reading a pet intelligence test, we timed how long it took our beloved Truffles to "Find the Hidden Treat." When we computed her score, it was clear Truffles was no Doggie Einstein, a fact I stopped my husband from noting aloud, *because there's no point hurting her feelings*. He looked at me like I'd lost my mind.

I'd hurt plenty of feelings during my teenage years and thankfully had learned along the way that kindness is a fundamental decency we owe to ourselves and to others.

Truffles might have forgiven or forgotten the verbal slight, but we humans always remember criticism. I raised my boys to be kinder than necessary, because people are not the dog.

Grace is a
multipurpose word,
contemplative
and positive.

Share . . . show . . .
say . . . grace.

You can never have too many aprons . . .

At a gas station in rural Georgia, the proprietor directed me "round back" for the ladies' facility. I feared a compromise to my plumbing standards, but the space was pristinely tiled and clean, with a waft of Pine-Sol in the air. Best of all, there were items to purchase displayed lovingly on the shelves along the wall—colored glasses, porcelain figures, and a stack of neatly folded aprons with price tags dangling from bitty safety pins. Eureka!

or too many memories.

I commemorated my discovery of the bathroom-with-shopping by purchasing the entire cache of aprons.

When my husband tells this story, he recalls it as the most expensive pit stop on record. My version is more about the serendipity of aprons being in that bathroom rather than hats or books. We have fond memories of that road trip in common. Aprons and memories. You can never have too many of either.

Hang your fantasy wardrobe right next to your real-life attire.

*I*n my closet are two sets of clothing: my Real-Life Attire and a Fantasy-Life Wardrobe. On most days, I wear an outfit that coordinates with my life as it is. But every so often, I zip into a confection more suitable for walking the red carpet than walking the dog, and then I go walk the dog!

15

Wearing an apron is just good sense.

> "During the Middle Ages, probably one of the biggest mistakes was not putting on your armor because you were 'just going down to the corner.'"
>
> —*Jack Handey*

An apron is domestic armor, shielding our clothing against the splatter and tatter of keeping house. Wear an apron and your guard is up.

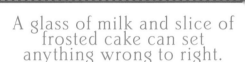

A glass of milk and slice of frosted cake can set anything wrong to right.

𝓘f something's a piece of cake, it's simple. For me, a piece of cake was always, literally, the simplest way to fix my boys' childhood and adolescent anguish. When one was cut from the team or lost a class election or left out of a party or wrongly disciplined (only wrongly) and kept after school: cake.

> **"It's a piece of cake."**
> **Slang:** Something that's easy and pleasurable to do.

I let him eat cake. Not a measured sliver of unfrosted pound cake, mind you, but a two-inch carving of yellow cake made three inches tall by the swirl of chocolate frosting on top and between the layers. And to wash each bite past the lump in his throat, there was always a tall glass of cold milk.

TIP: The cake can be store-bought, but the milk has to be cold.

Wear pearls with your apron and you're dressed up enough.

As a girl, I loved how Harriet Nelson and the other television moms dressed up to stay home and take care of a family. I imagined that I would one day be just like them, a homemaker in high heels, crinolines poufing the skirt of my shirtwaist, a belt to nip, an apron, and pearls. I got my stay-at-home-mom wish, but I tended my brood wearing jeans and faded T-shirts.

It's with some irony that I note the day I tied on a pretty apron, I felt prettier. I stood straighter and felt better about myself, too. Snapping the clasp on a strand of pearls, I was dressed up! To stay home.

Aprons + pearls = everyday chic.

When company's on the doorstep, it's amazing how much dusting an apron can accomplish in a matter of seconds.

The phone rings and unexpected company excitedly shares, "We're five minutes from ringing your doorbell." This is no problem, as my normal standards for a kempt hearth are about appearance, not depth.

How to tidy your home and become an insta-hostess—in

> "I make no secret that I would rather lie on a sofa than sweep beneath it.

three hundred seconds or less? Let me count the ways. There are five:

1. Grab and unfurl a heavy-duty garbage bag and, with utter abandon, toss into it everything that is cluttering your floors, furniture, and countertops. Throw the bag down the basement stairs or into the hall closet.

2. Yank apron over head and quickly dust all surfaces in the living room.

> But you have to be efficient
> if you're going to be lazy."
> —*Shirley Conran, British designer*

Toss dirty apron downstairs after the garbage bag.

3. From a kitchen drawer, locate the stash of emergency cosmetics. Apply blush and lip gloss, and brush hair into a neat ponytail.

4. Don a fresh apron from the ironed stack in the dining room buffet.

5. Breathless and maybe even barefoot, answer the door with a smile: "I'm so happy you called . . ."

Treat yourself like your own best company.

When I inherited my mother-in-law's china, crystal, and silver, the plates, glasses, and cutlery were over fifty-five years old but looked brand-new. "Oh," said my husband, "that's because she only put that stuff out when company was extra special."

"How often was that?" I wondered.

"Not very," he said. She entertained plenty, but her guests rarely warranted the "good" stuff.

Plenty of women in generations past saved the good china for just the right company and a best apron to wear only on special occasions. Who was good enough is the real mystery. Whoever it was didn't just call out of the blue or show up on the doorstep.

I use my mother-in-law's china every day, respectful of its beauty, of course, but with a nonchalance she would find shocking. If my everyday family isn't good enough for the good china, who is? Wait for the call from who is good enough, and you may never live long enough.

In a world of aprons, there's no such thing as too much rickrack.

On a tour through our friends' new home, we peeked into the bedroom and saw rows and rows of pillows lined up against the headboard. Rectangles. Squares. Circles. Bolsters in two sizes. *Rickrack*.

Rickrack, I thought as I stood in line behind a young woman with

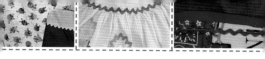

piercings upward of ten in each ear. *Rickrack*, I thought as I saw a car completely plastered with bumper stickers and a dog wearing rain gear.

Rickrack makes us happy and gives our humanity its finishing touch.

> "We must every one be a man of his own fancy."
> —*William Shakespeare*

"When the telephone rings, it's against the law not to answer it."
—*Ring Lardner*

Smile when you answer the phone. Your listener can hear a smile a thousand miles away.

A spotless apron
is like a photo
album with
no pictures.

Every smudge on your
apron is a stain of love,
holidays, and home. Collect
and savor them one and all!

Fear not
letting go the
apron strings.

"Sometimes the best way to hold
on to something is to let it go."
—Author unknown

The best way to hold on to children is to let them go. Sure, there are days when our young children take the stuffing out of us and we cannot wait for them to be off. But then they do leave, and the house is so silent we can hear the molecules banging about.

If we do it right and let our grown children experience living free from the tethers, they will come home.

Let the first
thing you
say brighten
someone
else's day.

Step into a Waffle House and the waitress stops whatever it is she's doing and calls out "Mornin'!"—the most welcoming of greetings. Imagine if we were all like Waffle House waitresses, taking the time to greet one another, strangers, too, with "Mornin'!"

Brightening someone else's day brightens your own day first.

> "Enjoy yourself. It's later than you think."
>
> —*Chinese proverb*

Live life as an exclamation point!

Celebrate the job you didn't get, the college you didn't get into, the spurned love, that awful haircut, because where we end up is where we're meant to be! Life is too short not to live it up.

Change directions often, and where you end up is anything but lost.

An occasional veer off the beaten path, a moment of spontaneity and risk, is perhaps your shortcut to something sublime. The worst that can happen is you'll be the fool—a temporary and survivable condition.

If your piecrust won't stick together, make cobbler instead.

With your apron and countertop covered in flour, roll out the top crust with a rolling pin (I always use my mother-in-law's green-handled one), setting it down when you judge the dough to be just the right thickness and size around.

Folding the dough in half
and then half again, ply the
crust from the counter and
maneuver it atop the filling.
When the gesture goes awry
and the dough rips and falls to the
countertop in pieces, there's no need
to panic. Gingerly place dollops of
crust on top of the pie filling,
bake as usual, and what
will emerge from your
oven is cobbler. And,
with generous spoons full

> "A crust eaten in peace is better than a banquet partaken in anxiety."
>
> —Aesop

of whipped cream, the cobbler will taste just like, well, pie!

TIP: Avoid baking bubble-over by cooking fruit in a saucepan with seasonings and thickener. Cool before adding to a bottom piecrust that's been painted lightly with egg white.

Happy is the household where laughter, music, kindness, and hospitality are in more abundance than little piles of this and that.

And that's where apron pockets come in handy! The disorder that finds its way into an apron pocket—lost pen caps, broccoli bands, magazine blow-in cards—can always be dealt with later!

Cleaning out a closet is as good as panning for gold.

Years ago, as we were leaving for a two-week trip, I took pains to hide one of my favorite and most valuable pieces of jewelry. I didn't bother to write myself a note about where the necklace was hidden because the spot

was so obvious. I haven't worn that
necklace since, because I have no
idea where it is!

Every now and then I go through
the closets one by one, checking
every shoe, boot, purse, pocket, and
cranny. I never find the necklace,
but I am always rewarded with
other treasures: a missing mother-
of-pearl formal cuff link, the pair
an anniversary gift to my husband;

a bright red clip-on bow tie my youngest wore at three; crumpled notes of faith, "Here is my tooth plese leve me $" and tattletale, "Mom I did not do it, Noah did it!"; a battered shoe box with unopened baseball card packets; a manila envelope of love letters to my teen heartthrobs, Dr. Kildare and Elvis. Sometimes, when you seek, the thing you find is better than what you were looking for.

New shoes don't pinch until you leave the store.

New shoes and new friendships are alluring. Captivated by a shiny new pump or a friendly face, I commit too quickly to the purchase or to telling my deepest secrets. Even when the fit isn't quite right, I'm convinced that with time, the shoes and the friendship *will give*. When the pinch doesn't subside, I take a while to admit error, then I go shopping again.

> "Even the most tempting rose has thorns."
>
> —*Tristan Eggener*

A bit of whimsy is a sweet pleasure that irons away at life's little wrinkles.

More sweet pleasures: singing along to Elvis, room service, a new appliance, an empty laundry basket, holding hands, lighting candles on a child's birthday cake, hearing a good joke and remembering it.

Learn to listen. Opportunity sometimes knocks softly.

How many times was I in the right place at the right time, but I didn't hear opportunity knocking because I was talking? Or thought I heard a rap-a-tat-tat, but was too insecure to believe the cadence might be meant for me?

I'd long since abandoned hearing
the sound of one hand clapping, when
one day I hung a bunch of aprons
on a clothesline, and in the slightest
wind, they began to dance and twirl.
Standing there in the backyard, I just
knew that the spirit of the women who'd
worn those aprons was trying to get my
attention, and if I really, really listened,
I would hear their voices. Opportunity
was a silent breeze.

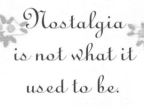

Nostalgia is not what it used to be.

"Happiness is good health and a bad memory."

—Ingrid Bergman

While a senior in college, my eldest son took a class on cultural anthropology. "Parent bashing" it should have been titled, for once into its studies, my firstborn reported to me that statistics did not bear out my memories of an idyllic '50s childhood. According to his required reading—books authored with dubious credentials, in my humble opinion—my memory is selective.

I don't even question whether he's right or not, because so what? No two people recall the same incident with identical details anyway.

Shaping a recollection to suit a sunnier or funnier version isn't the crime my son's college curricula claimed; it's choosing to look back to when my parents were alive, doing the best they could, cutting them slack, and calling those days happy ones.

Look sharp, feel smart.

Only you think no one notices that your pants are hemmed with duct tape.

Serve chips from the bag and hearts will sag.

My upbringing was a litany of repetitive instruction—sit up straight, get your hair out of your eyes, brush your teeth, go to bed, chew with your mouth shut, don't mumble, don't interrupt, because I said so, go to your room. At eighteen, I'd have chosen the fate of Anne Boleyn before I'd publicly tug at hiney-hiked underwear. There was also instruction on domestic proprieties: "A set table does not include food, liquid, or condiment in its store-bought packaging."

Growing up, I thought it dumb to empty potato chips from the bag into a bowl, pour milk from the carton into a crystal pitcher, and squirt catsup and mustard out of their plastic containers into matching ceramic ones, each with its own miniature silver spoon. We weren't to the manor born, so why all the fancy dancy? It wasn't until I was teaching my own children that I figured it out for myself: Niceties, the subtleties of civilized behavior, go a long way toward making less seem more.

Flowers on the table
are a must.

single daisy in a colored vase,
roses bunched in a soup can, or—
the favorite of children—dandelions

and grass blades in
a crystal punch cup,
flowers on the table
make even the simplest
meal special.

Once, with a light repast set and
guests impending, I realized I had no
flowers for the table and my own yard
was empty of blooms. Racing around
the neighborhood in search of flowers,

I knocked on the door of a home with
a profusion of blossoms in the yard.
Whether it was the lopping shears in
my hand or the ridiculousness of my
request to *borrow* some
flowers, I took home
a huge bouquet.
Never has a kitchen
sink salad received
such accolades.

There's no
substitute for
leather shoes and
a good haircut.

> "Believing in yourself and liking yourself is all a part of good looks."
>
> —*Shirley Lord*

Whether dressing to impress, dressing for success, or dressing up for a change, what we wear is less important than the timeless details of shined leather shoes and a decent haircut. Quality never goes out of style, nor should pride of self.

An apron is one of life's
necessities—but it makes
a nice accessory, too.

The best memories—
if not the best pies—are
the ones you create with
no planning.

My boys were four and two and
a half the day we decided to bake a
pie. Setting out the ingredients for an
old-fashioned apple pie, I envisioned
a memories-in-the-making, rainy-day

moment for the three of us. Positioned counter-height on stools, they looked so cute in Daddy's old shirts, buttoned up the back. Then the fighting began. They tussled over the dough, the rolling pin, the cookie cutters, the cinnamon, and the sugar shaker. They hit, they cried, they made a sticky mess. I thought cleaning up the chaos was surely what I would remember most.

When the clouds cleared, I

opened the back door to a yard
turned quagmire. The dog lit out first,
followed by my sons, who would put
their newfound culinary skills to task
in a mud-pie-making extravaganza.
Decorating with crushed leaves and
pebbles, they reveled in squishing and
shaping and baking their creations in
the dog's house, their make-believe
oven. Tie one on with a child and
make a pie—apple or mud!

A smile costs nothing and is beyond price.

On a trip to China, we were strolling through a park when it began to rain. Buckets. Umbrellas popped open all around us, and little groupings of men and women looked toward us and beckoned. I quickly took shelter with three women under

> "Everyone smiles in the same language."
>
> —Author unknown

one umbrella, and, huddled like four peas in a pod, our noses practically touching, we waited out the storm. My six-foot-three husband, a giant in China, stood beneath a canopy of a dozen raised umbrellas.

Walking back to our hotel after the downpour, I told him that the women and I spent our time together chatting about our children and husbands, our years married, our ages, our hair . . . "How in the world," he asked, "did you come to learn anything about them and not know a word of Chinese?" It sounds preposterous, I know, but we spoke through our smiles.

Nap often.

When my children were young, I had a rule: Unless the house is on fire, everyone takes a nap after lunch. They've long cut and run, but if there is one bit of childhood they would love to reclaim, it is napping midday. There's good reason for

their wistful longing: A nap is renewal. A nap is escape.

Forward-thinking employers may sanction a resting of the eyes midday, but never a nap, for the difference between a nap and a rest is when preparing for a nap, you take off your clothes and get into bed. Do try this at home!

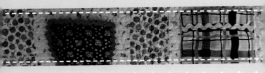

Folding laundry is the best meditation.

Any quiet activity that doesn't require your complete attention, like ironing or folding clothes warm from the dryer, is an experience so sweet smelling and therapeutic it's neglectful to our well-being not to do it more often.

71

We're not leaving until everybody goes winkytink.

*I*f you don't go, you're not going.
We're not stopping. I mean it.
Did you try? Well, try harder.
Now, don't you feel better?

"If at first you don't succeed, just do it like your mother told you."
—Author unknown